WALKING THROUGH SHADES - IN SEARCH OF LIGHT

RAJ DARJI

Believe in your Dreams!

Contents

Contents

Preface

Dear Reader,

Thank you so much for buying my book.

'Walking through Shades – In Search of Light' is my debut poetry book, consisting poems connected to each other representing the life of a dreamer.

The up's and down's, highs and lows which follows through the journey of life and how an individual overcomes this obstacles ending up victorious on his path. It is also a tribute to the loved one's who supported him, who forever stood by him in his journey.

I have tried my best to recite this fictional story in poetry format. I hope you connect and end up with my book making some space in your memory. The poems are really close to me and I am optimistic that they will strike a special chord with you too.

I wish you have a beautiful time reading.

Regards,

Raj Darji

Acknowledgements

'Walking through Shades – In Search of Light', my book, would not be possible without the support of many of people in my life.

I would like to thank my family who stood by me each step of my way. Their faith helped me keep working on my craft. The amount of strength they provided to my wings played a crucial role in my flight.

My friends who acted as the biggest driving force in this journey. They were the first one's who read my poems and stories. They critiqued me the best way possible.

My school teachers who guided me in my frame of art, they went through my work and enhanced my writing skills. A dear thanks to 'Creative Writing Modern Age (CWMA)' group where I met a lot of writers across the globe. I shared my work and gained a lot of knowledge.

A special thanks to 'Furknsaglam'. The cover picture of this book has been clicked by him, which I availed through the 'Pexel app'.

Lastly, the entire team of 'Notion Press Publishers' I will always be grateful to you. Thank you for the trust you have displayed in my book. The journey of publishing my first book would not be possible without you.

Thank you so much everyone!

Prologue

The poems revolve around the phenomenon of 'Life'. Our individuality, our individual fear's; Instances which have formed a great impact with our way of thinking and perceiving this world. On our journey from a child, naive and unaware of reality, always been taken care with love and belonging. To growing up, feeling emptiness within crowd, asked to adapt in a blink.

Understanding responsibilities which come with time, the rising need to take a particular decision. Finding it tough to process, eventually debating and just blatantly arguing, still not finding any answer. To simply pursue our dream even tougher then succeeding taking it further. A step of bravery towards dream and every second, filling your yard with questions, we try to answer them all and things remain the same with more blame sticking to our name.

The state of unconsciousness and feeling lost, getting supported by a person, a part of the crowd where everyone is laughing at you, standing apart with a smile showcasing belief. No mystery, no layers, an open book with nothing to hide. Not a riddle to decipher, just the beauty of nature to admire. Holding hands being bold with broader outlook to fly, leaving 'W's' and just smiling whenever with each other. Solutions start appearing, problem begin to disappear.

Walking every day, working on our path, where things are not changing but you believe to bring that change. Heading with faith, the only way fate is going to come into play. Hurdles cuddling and building more burdens, we stay awake, outdoing our self-everyday with work. Finally, a little hope of light to strengthen our drop shoulders. Praying and wishing for things to fall into place.

Years of hard work replacing tears with happiness. My desire's getting fulfilled with dream coming true. Tying knot with that special person, bridging gaps. A new chapter we start together. My life was changing with those horrible laughs turning to bliss of smile having reasons behind it. Now, I was never left alone, there were always people around me. But, I did not see thunder striking with rain.

I found no control over myself, intoxicated with success. I was on cloud nine and losing my contact with everyone on the grounded level. I was hanging at a great height with pride. I was covering my sadness with mask. Soon, I fall with God's grace however I didn't face any harm because a protective cushion of my dear one's was there to protect. The phase I had passed was back, to test me again. I started self-destruction because of my complex state of mind and emotions.

My dear one's helped me with comfort and care. I did not know what was left in the mystery box of life? But that was enough for me to re-analyze and reconstruct my broken life. If I can do it once, I can make it happen again, I assured myself it will happen and I did it. Through this period, I kept learning how a person keeps re-learning from various incidents that keep flowing, showing you different colors of life. I am satisfied with this life with my partner right next to me. At present, I only wish to leave everything and rest in God's vicinity.

Though, I have understood one thing about life that you can't understand it.

Poems

The Narrow Lanes

1. 12 A.M. Talks

Will I ever be successful in my life?
Or a failure for everyone, to derive,
I cry in close corners, where no one resides,
Unable to confide my fear to anyone, I deny.

Failures are a part of everyone's life,
They come with a meaning, for one to understand,
Mistakes to rectify and restart your journey,
Giving a tough fight and not getting undermined.

Why I don't think conventionally?
Like everyone else; my parents being tensed,
About my future, questions they want answers,
Resulting in constant debate, inside my head.

Being different isn't a sin, never considerate.
It's your individuality that you possess,
And your effort can only help you to build a career,
Give time to your parents, things take time to process.

Still, I doubt was taking Arts a good choice?
Was commerce a good option considering money?
Fulfilling dream a phenomenon only for films,
Harsh is the fact hence called reality.

Taking decision is tough, though we have to,
It may fall short, it may fall right, you can't decide that,
You can only keep working on your craft till perfection,
Dreams do come true in reality, if you dare and keep faith.

I must sleep, it's late night and the sky is dark,
Hope everything goes well and bring some bright light,
I become capable enough to serve my parents a good life,
A better future waiting for me, until then good night.

2. Darkness Bringing Light

Under moon and stars, my closed eyes are painting dreams,
Travelling me to a fairytale land away from this world its noise and scream.

An entire day ending, while my life getting entertained with his own grief,
Happiness surrounds me only at night, where I can accept myself, though brief.

I'm not fit to be a morning person, because there's always a lot to remember what's wrong and what's right,
At night, I can serve my time to passion, and there wouldn't be anyone to judge, everything will be alright.

Humans being sad with a mask on their face, we witness fake smiles,
With the setting sun, it becomes difficult to hold, we still continue, justifying life rhyming with lie.

Brightness brings positivity to drive hence we keep running
in life for work or from our life towards night,
Alone enjoying some time few smiles and tears to
compliment, feeling free to be myself, darkness bringing
light.

3. Childhood

Gazing this world, admiring it, through my small eyes,
Unaware that everything on this land has a price.
Getting aspired from the people surrounding me,
Cultivating a dream, an inspiration for others to be.
Witnessing people running behind every penny of money,
Somewhere, the beauty of nature was getting lost entirely.
Like a seed, I was being nurtured with care and blessings,
Growing up imbibing all those qualities, creating a tracing.
Maturity coming with time, making it tough to just be a child.
Moving forward, understanding the need and craft to hide.
Expectations made his way; burden came along as a friend,
We are always asked to mold ourselves with the changing trend.
From being a free living and special person in the house,
Turning to lost and fearful of everything, filled with doubts.
Soon childhood got over with its innocence,
Future and thoughts regarding it came into existence.

4. Conflcit

I am having a conflict with my own self,
Over my looks, my weight, my body and its shape,
The clothes which I wear,
More than often I just don't get my perfect size,
Shouldn't be tight and lose clothes don't look good,
And yes, I am aware, but I don't know what I should do?
To pursue what my brain commands? Or believe in what my heart feels?
Somewhere, I am giving a lot of importance to what people think about me, talk about me,
Sometimes, I want to get rid of everything and don't give a single thought about anyone's opinion,
But, I also want to hear them and self-interrogate,
To correct everything within and just be perfect,
So that, people don't find any flaws,
They don't judge me or categorize me of a particular section,
Doesn't it sound stupid of me?
'It does!' My heart responds,
'You are just being practical and there's nothing wrong with it!' My brain recites,
Why I can't just be happy with the fact that I love myself?
It's weird, I know,
Sadly, true, we all know and guilty, a part of!

5. Standing At Crossroad

When routes diversify and mistakes start getting amplify,
We stand at crossroads, to mold ourselves with the phase passing by,
Getting curbed in a cocoon, a black hole for existence,
For construction of destruction,
Eliminating risk and failure, acting as a savior of our own life,
Wishing for death to surrender with pride in everyone's eye.

Or stand at crossroads, accepting failures, rectifying mistakes,
To absorb that water with all the impurities,
To penetrate discomfort with luxuries, through constant efforts,
Ending may be victorious or sadly you might fail, but you won't curse fate,
Taking all the pleasure of your decision,
In recognition of that moment, you might start celebration.

Standing at crossroads you derive your future,
Combined by fear and ambition you drive further,
With dedication and attention to details you win your fights,

Reaching to end of your journey and sleepless nights,
Deepen more satisfaction with roots being attached to ground,
End of those lonely hours in dark room, now everyone is around.

My Grey Surroudning

6. Silence

Silence we encounter, submerged in sorrow,
Constant debacles hindering my way to succeed,
With no access to support, my life is hollow,
Whatever efforts I put, a step behind I am, failure is always in lead.

❧❧❧

Silence we deal, when unanswerable questions arrive,
They enquire about our past and future, leaving our present depressed,
With zero guides to help us defend this question, we are left deprive,
Speculation keeps on increasing, decreasing our interest in life and people won't be surprised.

❧❧❧

Silence we proclaim, we want from people with useless judgments,
They wish us to surrender our personality and perspective,
We act like fools, by analyzing each statement and rethinking of every moment,
We scream, we want them to shut but sadly they are always active.

Silence we inhale, when difficult situations comes at our door step,
It feels like death, because no one accompanies us,
Even the closest might be unavailable to help and enemies would be ready with knife to stab,
Getting stumbled in web, unknown of our next move, feeling lost.

7. Parallel

The truth is whispering,
But there is sound of lie.
A person willing to express,
Is stopped by us, why?
If you can't digest love,
Abhorrence is alright.
Colors are all fatal,
Darkness is true light.
Numerous thought collides,
And leaves one deprive.
Humans wish to see themselves,
And the mirror leaves them in surprise.
We wish for a better world,
But at the end we all sleep with our closed eyes,
This place is parallel from our imagination,
It can be unparalleled; it's we, where the change resides.

8. An Eye filled with Dreams

An eye filled with dreams,
Is drowning out of tears.

I am burden to my thoughts,
Who never find a way to escape.
They evolve with time,
Or decay falling short to survive.

I wish death had a course,
I might have a better chance to die.

I want to believe in destiny,
While its existence never lied in my sphere!
Because a believer of faith,
Ended up in sad demise.

A little satire to make my life happy,
While smile is a part of attire.

9. Melancholy

It was not yesterday when he came,
It might not be tomorrow when he will leave.

I think the reason is my smile,
That brings him to my life.

He surrounds me in an empty room,
Through my tears he confirms everything is good.

My days are dark I argue for light,
Stars in night are invisible for my delight.

Certainly I am burden by the people in crowd,
We all have same face or it's a mirror which is bestowed.

One day I broke my shackles and ran out,
I was standing at a sea shore; I came back town.

On my way back I understood,
Melancholy is here to stay without a doubt.

10. Burning Flames

I see burning flames of my desire,
And unwillingly I have lit that fire,
At the dawn of my eclipse I conspire,
Regardless of my efforts, I fall short to succeed and inspire.

In burning flames, I see my memories turning to ash,
Everyone running a race, flipping sides to win, in a splash,
I am still discovering life and filling some incomplete space,
Dealing with sorrows; arriving at my place.

I lost my smile; I threw it in burning flames,
To bring an end to my fakeness and unwanted claims,
Giving freedom to myself, to express and accept with no shame,
No pressure to get appreciated by everyone, just focusing on my aim.

10 Burning Places

Assimilation of Time

11. Good or Bad, To Stay Alive Or be Dead

Just a blank thought and few outdated lines,
A blank skate in my hand, fully black, like my life.

A day sitting in dark light over viewing my decisions,
Overthinking why I am different? With so many unanswered questions?

Walking everyday on same routes, offering to me nothing new,
With my shoulders dropped down, moments to cherish are very few.

A life filled with failures with my handful of achievements,
I tilted towards pen on a journey full of amusement.

I don't have any idea what's good or bad,
Better or worse unaware, whether to stay alive or be dead.

12. Forever Stay

My unheard silence never found your way,
At a distance, I always stayed away,
I thought many times to hold your hand,
Look into your eyes and tell you whatever I wish to say,
But every time, I held myself back,
I waited for years for that one single day,
Where I could confide my feelings for you,
And find a place in your life where forever I could stay…
Life took a huge turn when you called me one fine day,
You had something important to say,
I thought this is the moment I should end this play,
When we met you told me someone has proposed you,
And your answer is 'Yes' I smiled in great enthusiasm,
But the only thing I felt was deep sorrow enduring my grave,
Don't worry, my unheard silence will never find your way,
Silence which whisper 'I Love You' impact in my life will forever stay…

13. Disturbed Life, Undefined Scares

Disturbed life, undefined scares,
Memories to erase, forever present marks,
Under dark moon light, we seek stars,
Realizing that our destination is still too far…

Hurdles and obstacles blend with us,
Like those evil nights when devil applause,
Curbing ourselves in silence we are lost,
For courage to uplift, we find fate to change our clause…

Unheard or told to keep quiet,
There is always a fine line to differentiate,
Whether we are alive or a puppet,
Controlled by someone, tied with threads, in debt…

14. Left

Being left alone by someone you love can be perplexing,
Hard to find a way to forget and move on,
The memories and time you shared together start appearing,
Reminding you how much you cared about each other, once.
Finding some way to rebuild that relationship,
Constantly trying to talk to that person, finding a minute to apologize,
To reanalyze the decision of breaking up, to realize the reason of companionship,
Drawing out possibilities and figuring out differences.
Or might just accept the fact, the reality of life,
It will take time for you to get over that phase,
But, you have to, willingly or unwillingly, stay alive,
Understanding life and facing its cruel knife.

15. Everything

Our emotions being locked and arrest, we feel numb,
We keep adjusting trying to feel alright, while life plays pun,
I assume an overdose fight with mirror will make me feel fine,
On the contrary, it leaves me bleeding every time.

I request myself to stay alive, to fight till the very end,
But most of the times, I lose hope and keep finding rest to bind,
Life is like a lime, I try to add sugar to enrich my sweetness,
However life only taste's sour because of my tears, crying every time.

Animosity is grave, visible in every one's eye,
Still people try to hide, unable to understand what they try to imply?
No true faces in the crowd, available to find,
The merciless journey of life continuous discarding whatever happens, every time.

Sound of New Waves

16. Dear Someone Special

Dear Someone Special,

.

With years of friendship we have together,
Some glorious memorizes we have created,
Smiles and tears have been a part of our journey,
Always stayed with each other, in our good and bad times,
Some feelings, never expressed, left in a corner, by my side,
In fear of things getting worse and more complex,
To never be able to get things back on track, staying true to one another,
Over burdening myself with thoughts and speculations,
Unable to find peace of mind, once chord of love hits the right note,
Yes, I Love You, even after a thousand reason for you to reject me,
To find a better pair, hundreds of things for you to tolerate inside me,
I couldn't stop myself, expressing my love for you.

.

Yours Truly, Best friend.

17. Dear Best Friend

Dear Best Friend,

.

Our friendship and understanding isn't that weak to be broken so easily,
Through this uncontrollable rush of emotions,
The bond we share is meant to last till the very end,
We are still left with many more smiles and tear to share together,
We both being introverts, have found our place of wisdom with each other,
Over the years, we have grown simultaneously,
And have developed habits, which only we recognize about both of us,
You acting completely idiotic in a room, pretending to be funny,
With your dead sense of humor, you are aware of,
Sometimes getting angry at me, when I do silliest things and harm myself,
Still taking care of mine, whenever I fall ill,
Every single things seems unnecessary and unimportant for you,
I enjoyed every bit of those moments,

You being horrible at hiding your emotions and lying to me at my face,
I knew everything you mentioned in that letter,
Sorry, I didn't help you and made things simpler,
But yes, 'I Love You' and I cannot imagine my life without you,
Hope you bear with me your entire life.

.

Yours Forever, Someone Special.

18. Miracle

Waiting for miracle to happen,
Working to make miracle happen…

A fine line which defines,
Your urge to up rise or decline,
Demanding patience your desire,
Demise will forever be the ultimate truth,
Only your actions will make you reach,
Your destination, just don't lose faith.

Waiting for miracle to happen,
Working to make miracle happen…

A battle to combat within our own self,
We have to act like a fox in this world full of wolf,
Adapting with situation but not ending up as a dwarf,
Things working at once might not at another,
Blunders will happen to know how good you are as a learner,
Life won't help you with service in cold, providing a jacket of leather.

Waiting for miracle to happen,
Working to make miracle happen…

Don't disservice your work with lies,
To change how people, look at you through their eyes,
Traces won't help you to justify your acts, wise or otherwise,
Always remember, there is price on everyone's head,
Trust won't guarantee truth and people will act deaf,
With the day ending, if nothing works everything is just a bluff.

Waiting for miracle to happen,
Working to make miracle happen…
You decide!

19. Relationship

When true love resides between two souls,
Boundless compassion and emotion truly last,
Smile's forever on their face, they mostly talk with their eyes,
They stay with each other's memories, when apart,
Both of them missing each other, desperate to be together,
To spend some close time once reunite,
Speak about feeling broken,
The space, time had brought in our life,
Few more seconds to spend together changing to hours long discussion,
With some stupid, little fights,
To breathe together, appreciating each other's company,
Certainly, not thinking about time any more,
Saying 'I Love You' once more, enriching sweetness in relationship,
Just living and capturing those moments for the rest of our life...

20. Divinity in Vicinity

Air whispering, passing through my ears,
Memories, I wish to erase are drowning me in tears.
I had belief in faith, soon I lost, and evident was fate,
In a queue, I was standing always been asked to wait.
Shattered in pieces, offering trouble, disguised with life,
Every single statement was false; I found my life a big lie.
Devastated is my present, tired struggling with past,
Still, my hope for better future is breathing, I am unaware,
how long it's going to last.
I want to quit and rest in peace with my life being surrender,
But I am weak, I simply can't, instead I write to find answers.
I feel, divinity in vicinity, whenever I write,
Unfortunate things happening, I believe will turn alright.

Surrendered to the Sky

21. Walking Miles

I have been walking miles,
With my feet asking me,
'Is your destination still alive?'

My eyes filled with dreams,
I desire to conquer them,
Regardless of the obstacles,
Life brings with time,
I have nothing to consider,
Apart from my wish to fly high.

I have been walking miles,
With my feet asking me,
'Is your destination still alive?'

I keep walking on my path,
I keep working on my craft,
Believing in my hard work,
And fate preparing my draft,
Things will turn the way I want,

Those days are not too far.

I have been walking miles,
With my feet asking me,
'Is your destination still alive?'

People do find me selfish at times,
And I try not to care,
But few things are just not in our control,
I prepare myself for the task, I dare,
Win or lose, I accept both of them,
I do feel disheartened; I cope up with smile.

I have been walking miles,
With my feet asking me,
'Is your destination still alive?'

Sometimes my shoulders drop,
I feel lost with no hope or faith,
Things start getting blur for me,
Such situations are tough but I have to face,
I stop for a second to garner,
All my spirit and strength.

I have been walking miles,
With my feet asking me,
'Is your destination still alive?'
I reply them with a smile,
'Yes, my destination is alive,
Soon to be my reality in this life.'

22. Things Falling into Place

The circle of life completing its circulation,
Years of hard work delivering its fruit,
Inheriting wisdom of satisfaction,
Whispers of appreciation I wished turning truth.

Fear of failure diminishing through faith,
Accomplishing my desire,
Surrounding myself with love no hate,
Feeling peace inside, calming my igniting fire.

Feathers to fly high, I felt,
With freedom from expectations after succeeding,
Trail of melancholy, I dealt,
Only sweetness is there, left in my surrounding.

Changing time has brought some ups and downs,
Tears are replaced with smile on my face,
Happiness has served me with a crown,
I have found a new life with things falling into place.

23. She Understood Everything

Having a beautiful walk with my someone special,
A ring kept in my hand for her,
I was thinking to propose her that night,
But my courage wasn't helping me out to the fullest.
Talking about various things I was fumbling,
She sensed something somewhere wrong with me,
And decided to stay quiet, watching me biting my nails,
YouTube tutorials were seriously not working for me that day.
Taking deep breathes; I tried to maintain eye contact,
For most of the part I did and faltered even as well,
Silence felt absurd with reason behind it,
I was ready for disapproval in my head but my heart wanted 'Yes'.
I told her, 'I Love you'; she replied, 'I Love you too',
For infinite times we had repeated this line for each other,
However, this time I was just messing around,
She held my hand and said, 'Give me that ring and a beautiful kiss'.
With nothing said from my end, she heard everything,
That night remains vibrant in my memory and its beauty,
We informed our parents the same night,
Happiness enriched between us and did spread.

24. If you wish...

If you wish, you can fulfill your dreams,
Just be ready to strive and give your work the required time,
Be patient because things don't happen overnight,
It takes those efforts from your side to covert,
Your work transforming from a beginner to expert and still working on your craft.

If you wish, you can stay happy forever,
But it's important for you to know yourself and live that way,
The smallest of help you offer might bring a smile,
And the priciest gift would never really satisfy you,
It's the way you look at life and seek happiness every time.

If you wish, you can aspire and inspire others,
But for that you should be your biggest motivation in life,
You should be in complete sense of your actions and always be true to yourself,
There will be moments of dissatisfaction and complete anguish,
Where you have to act wisely and take decision timely.

If you wish, you can discard judgments from your life,
Just focus on your work and pass a smile to those people,
Keep improving every day, learning something new,
Breaking out with your work, getting things right and let that moment speak for you,
The people won't rest and hesitate to add luck to your hard work, pass a beautiful smile again and your work is done.

25. A New Chapter

A New Chapter in my life is starting today,
Tying knot with her, 'someone special',
Heading towards a new journey,
I am ready to welcome all the arrival,
Of two routes getting submerged into one,
Leading to different outcomes.
To fulfill every oath, we take today,
I am always with you as your support,
A cushion for you to hold tightly,
Everlasting presence of comfort,
Between both of us, to share everything,
To accept every wrong and right thing.
Getting more time to talk and cherish,
To curse, 'I could've found someone better!'
Deep inside well aware, it's a lie,
And we are just perfect for each other,
Growing old with passing time,
Falling more in love with age flowing fine.

Yet Undefined

26. Changing Life

Life is like a stand-up comedy,
Where earlier everyone was laughing at me,
Now, they are smiling with me and there's reason behind it,
Today, they are clapping their hands and applauding me,
Appreciating and wishing me for many more achievements,
More glory to my crown with years to come.

A hostage life, my hostile surrounding,
Left me pounding and bounding to circumstances,
With I being agile to demonstrate my imagination,
And deconstruct my failures where there was a lot to learn,
I went from one stage to another to end up here,
Today I am standing at that place where you are stalking your success.

I was done and broke, there was no one to confide,
With every statement I used to hear sounded like a pun to my ear,
And I was alone to bear the burden of those words,
Initially, it made be resilient and tough to conquer the dust,
Today when they hear me, they find me arrogant,

Just because of their irrelevance.

Demise was desire, at once feeling shit of my own self,
A garbage bin was doing a better job, they made me feel,
I never spell this words but I did spit on my face,
I was lost and found hope on ground to work till I drown,
To make a mark of which everyone is proud,
Today I look back with pride when I see crown on my head.

27. Clouds - Surrounding Me!

Clouds - Surrounding me!
I felt there was no binding to me,
At top of everyone, I fell short to feel my feet,
My passion driving me, making me inattentive,
Of my actions, leading to destruction…

Clouds - Surrounding me!
I forgot, how to balance the cycle of life,
My work taking everything back from me,
The luxury it brought with time stayed at the same place,
Being the only ones left to talk with…

Clouds - Surrounding me!
I lost people surrounding me; I'm only left with clouds,
I came a long way carving my life with smiles,
Horribly, I don't see my dear ones truly smiling, being happy,
Maybe, my presence meant something to them…

Clouds - Surrounding me!

People see a successful person, neither the failure,
Not the loser, hiding inside, bribing mask,
To stay with him and last, because I see a person,
In the mirror, about whom nobody wants to ask for or see…

Clouds - Surrounding me!
It feels like dying with rope tied to my neck,
Hanging from a height with pride,
God cut that rope one day and I was falling on the ground,
A cushion filled with love saved me…

Clouds - No more around me!
My dear ones surround me every moment,
Together with me to conquer the tide,
Gearing up for the second innings,
Boosting my spirits and unleashing my happiness…

28. Still Learning...

I am walking with a crowd of people,
Some are my friends, while some just pretend,
I tend to believe I understand human beings,
Incidents have taken place where I was proven wrong,
I took my lesson and never walked back that route,
Though, I have faltered, I altered it with craft,
I'm on my quest to identify humans and my true friends,
Still learning…

Victory, the ultimate wisdom to conquer,
I wander in search of happiness,
Falling short to honor and respect my self,
Trying to fit in this world, typing myself unfit,
Creating hate and then finding love,
In this unlovable world with unavoidable grief,
Trying to plant a seed of love for myself,
Still learning…

Anguish and distress followed me,
Each step of my way and till date appears often,
Surprising me, as an unwanted guest,

I forgot my smiley face I had when I was a kid,
Reasons were not required for me to be happy,
Now, there are various occasions,
Where people want to see me smile,
Still learning…

We stay in a cage and worship freedom.
Enduring darkness expression of anguish,
Existence getting extinct, staying in past, which forever remains,
With our present, entitled to our future,
Un-freedom acting like a solvent to the drink called life,
Forever walking, treadmill at my feet,
Adapting this condition enhancing acceptance,
Still learning…

I don't know the end of this journey,
The end of my sorrow, my striving and my hiding,
The joy of life bringing some kind of hope,
Making me alive and richer with strength to begin,
Again and complete the half tale,
To make a comeback and commence never ending stay,
What is life and what he has left for me?
Still learning…

29. Present

Things got better for me after my free fall,
My dear one's who helped me at my worst,
I felt blessed with tears because they made me smile,
It was because of them I could fight standing tall.

I'm no more a burden, I have lost but I conquered,
My dream is my reality I have walked miles for that,
I had faith to work on, never allowed fate to decide,
God stayed with me, I thank Him being a believer.

'I Love You' and I will always do, till I stay alive,
For the trust you had in me, which kept me going,
Those moments of hug and intimacy we had,
Provided much require comfort to my uncomfortable life.

Someone Special, we forever stay in bliss,
Keep holding each other's hand, we never get divided,
I keep listening to you for endless hours you speak,
Our life is reducing every day; we shouldn't forget to kiss.

The life has finally completed its circle in my part,
The journey has been satisfying with lights getting dime,
I've seen many things few unwanted,
Still they remain close to me, I host them with craft.

At conclusion, I am standing with verdict at one end,
My eyes feel heavy and I look addicted to everyone,
It's true I want to disclose, not with drugs but to death,
My body needs rest; please take me God in your hands.

30. Life

Life is a box filled with mystery where people are busy finding victory,
Happiness comes with money and a good life is filled with luxury.
We articulate to justify and hide, not to express our true side,
In this world there is no space, leaving the one you make with pride.
We have to lift responsibilities of things as we grow with time,
Moments of sugar sweetness, life filled with sourness of lime.
In stress of our future, our present becomes thin air we breathe,
For this world, never allowing us to sleep; leaving us awake to weep.
Life keeps taking things away from us, ruthless stays its behavior,
With us, until we understand that it's because of us, we human creatures.

30. Life

About The Auhtor

Raj Darji is a budding writer, poet, blogger and a student. He is 17 years old and lives in Mumbai. Writing is his prime medium to communicate. 'Walking through Shades – In Search of Light' is his debut poetry book. Before this book, he has been co-author of 5 anthology books. He is select writer of 'Split Poetry India'. 'One of You' is the name of his writing page on Instagram. 'Gush of Thoughts' is the name of his blogger page. Connect with him:

Email id - imrd54321@gmail.com

Instagram - @_one.of.you

Just the beginning...

9 798886 419146

Printed by Libri Plureos GmbH in Hamburg, Germany